THE DIFFERENT AI ROBOTS AND THEIR USES

SCIENCE BOOK FOR KIDS
CHILDREN'S SCIENCE EDUCATION BOOKS

BABY PROFESSOR
EDUCATION KIDS

Speedy Publishing LLC
40 E. Main St. #1156
Newark, DE 19711
www.speedypublishing.com
Copyright 2017

In this book, we're going to talk about the different types of artificial intelligence robots and their uses. So, let's get right to it!

WHAT IS A ROBOT?

A robot is a machine that has special functions. It can carry out a complicated series of actions. A person can program the computer to tell the robot what to do. Computer programs can also do things based on what a human being tells them to do, but most people think of a robot as performing some type of physical motion for us.

TOY ROBOT

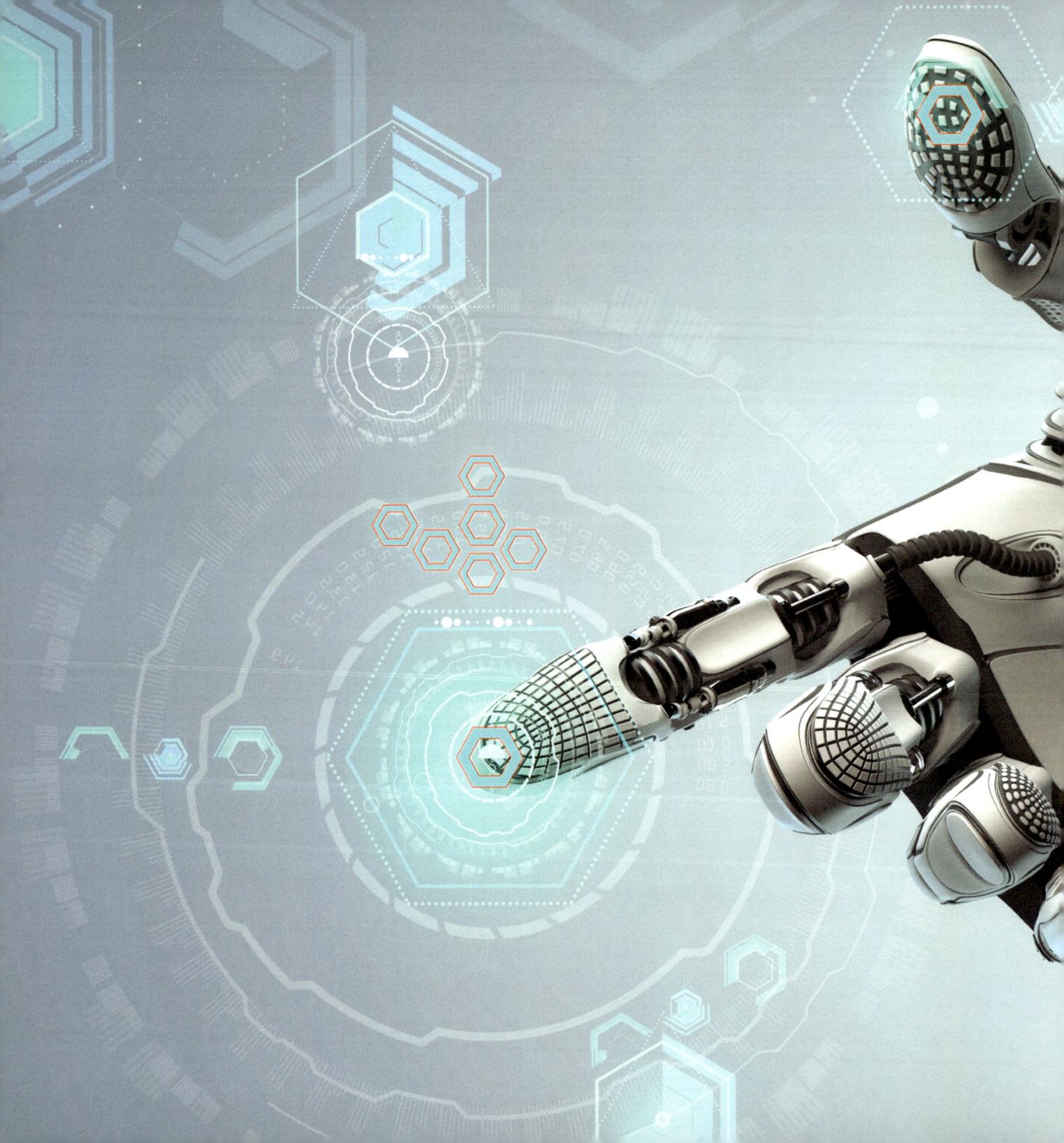

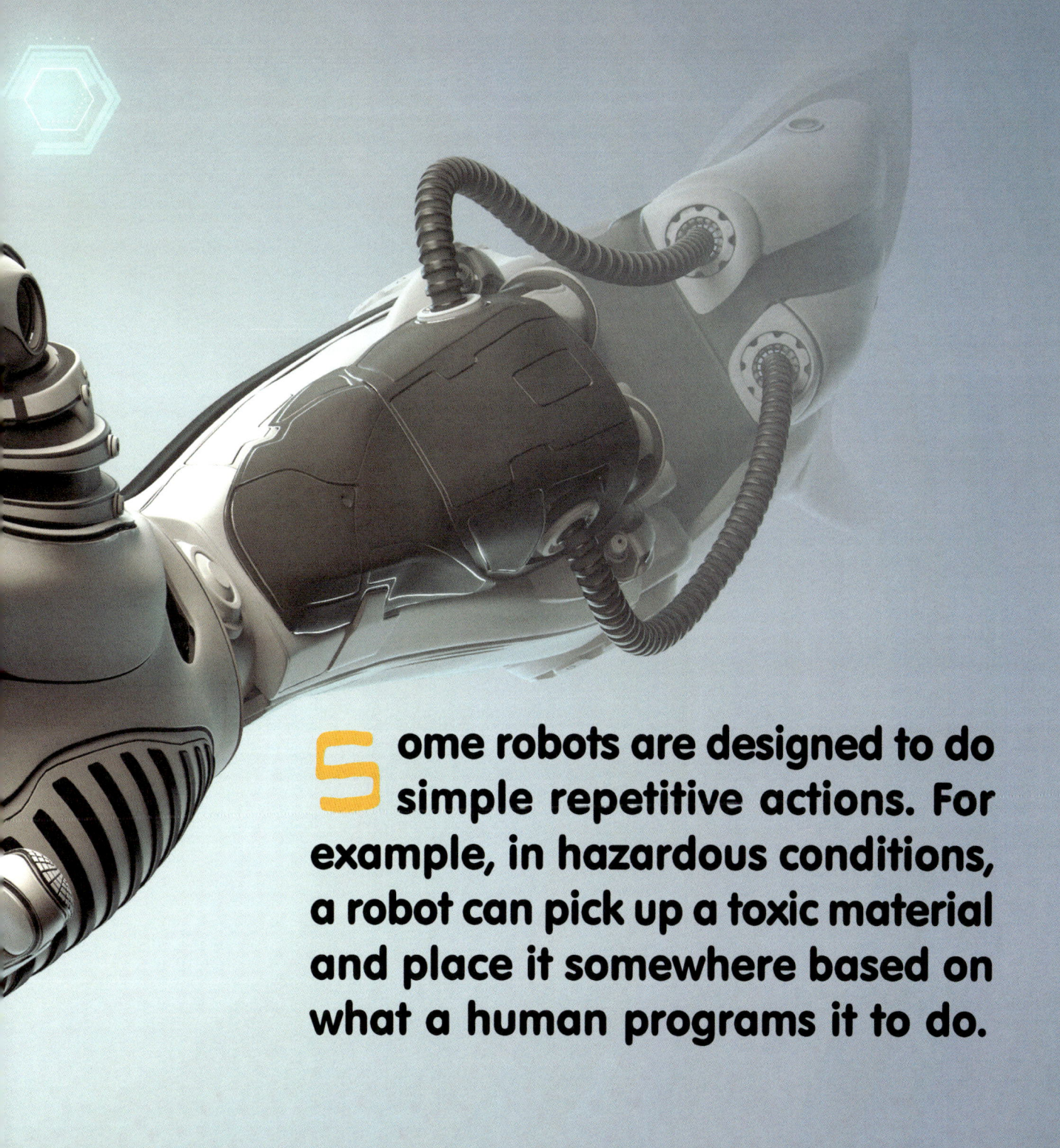

Some robots are designed to do simple repetitive actions. For example, in hazardous conditions, a robot can pick up a toxic material and place it somewhere based on what a human programs it to do.

Robots perform lots of work in assembly lines that human beings used to do. Industrial robots on a car assembly line can place bolts or screws into a car frame automatically. These types of robots generally just look like mechanical arms. They don't have a human appearance at all. However, robots with a "human" look have been discussed in science fiction for a long time and they are well on their way to becoming science fact.

ROBOTIC ARM FOR PACKING

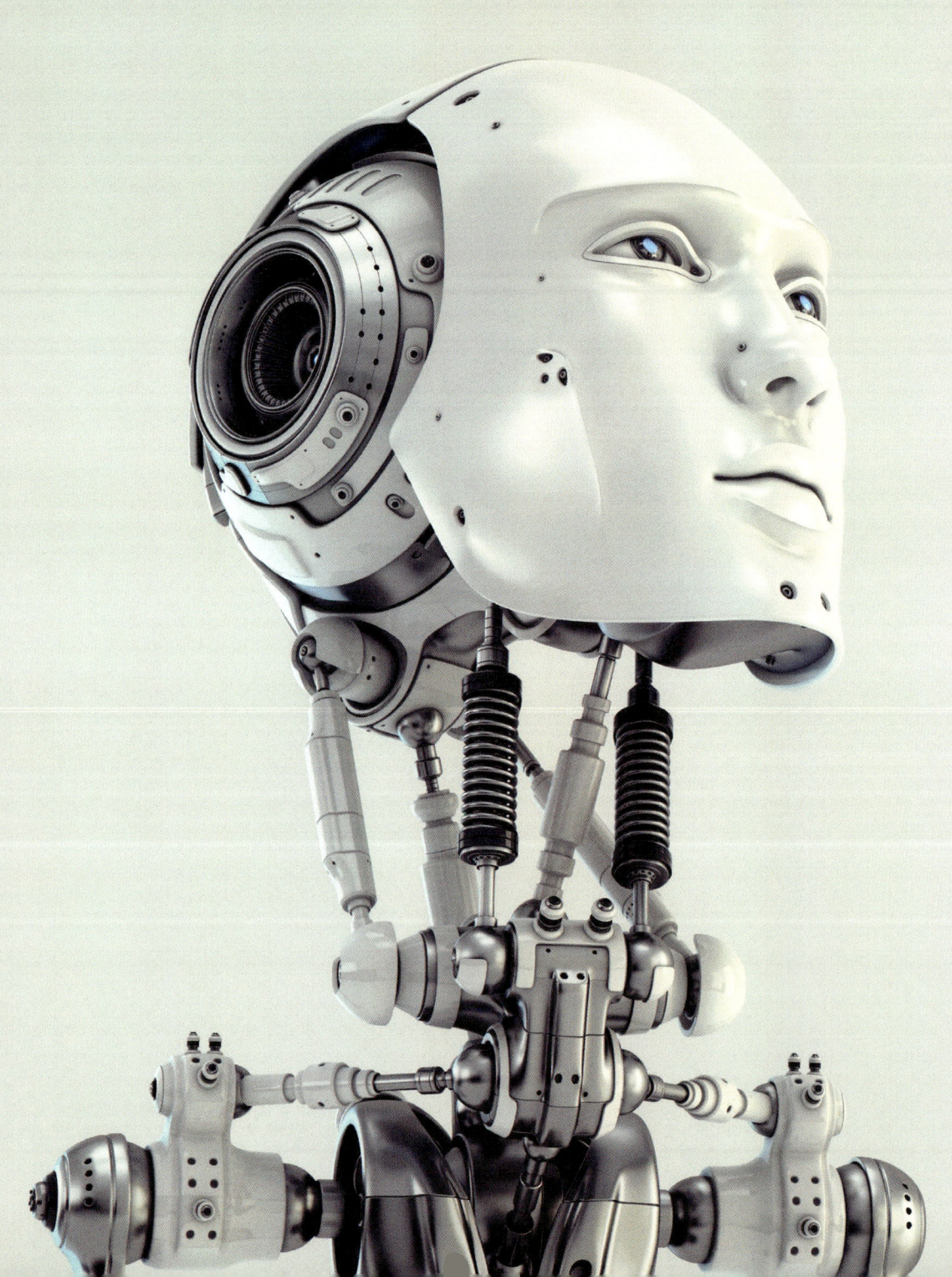

Scientists who create robots and work with them are called roboticists. Roboticists are not content with just building a robot model that looks like a person. They want to create robots that are as intelligent as or more intelligent than human beings. Some people are worried that if we build robots this intelligent they'll take over all the jobs that people do now.

WHAT IS ARTIFICIAL INTELLIGENCE?

Artificial Intelligence, called AI for short, is the development of computer systems and ultimately robots that can perform tasks that usually require human intelligence. Perceiving through seeing, understanding speech, making decisions that reduce risk, and translating between human languages are all functions that a computer or robot would have if it were fully intelligent with artificial intelligence.

In science fiction, there are robots that have the ability to learn anything. They can learn languages and they can think logically as well as solve problems just like a human being does. Many science fiction books and movies show robots that not only reason, but also create their own unique, original thoughts and ideas. Roboticists are not yet close to creating a robot that would be able to generate its own creative thoughts. However, they are making progress with programming robots to have some elements of human intelligence.

CAN ARTIFICIAL INTELLIGENCE ROBOTS SOLVE PROBLEMS?

Computers and robots can already solve some types of problems on their own. The idea of how they can solve problems isn't difficult, but getting them to do it well is. The computer or robot will get information about a certain situation through its own robotic sensors or from a human providing the data.

WOMAN ASSEMBLING OPTIC SENSOR FOR INTELLIGENT ROBOT SYSTEM

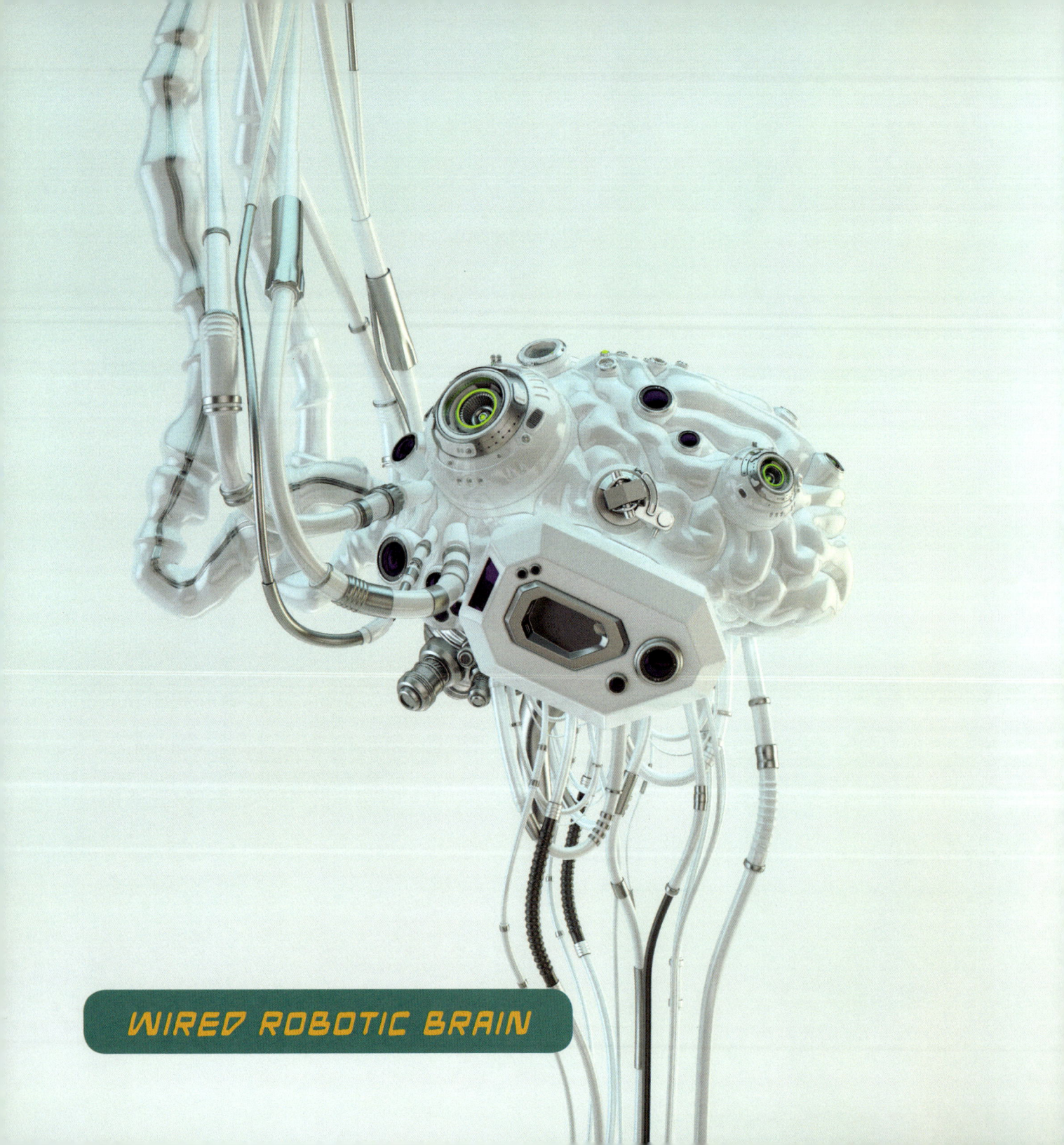

WIRED ROBOTIC BRAIN

The computer or robotic "brain" then compares this new situation to information that exists in its stored data to decide how the problem can be solved.

Then, it quickly goes through the possible actions it could take and makes a prediction about which action might have the chance for the greatest success. This type of rapid processing is something that computers and the robots they control do extremely well.

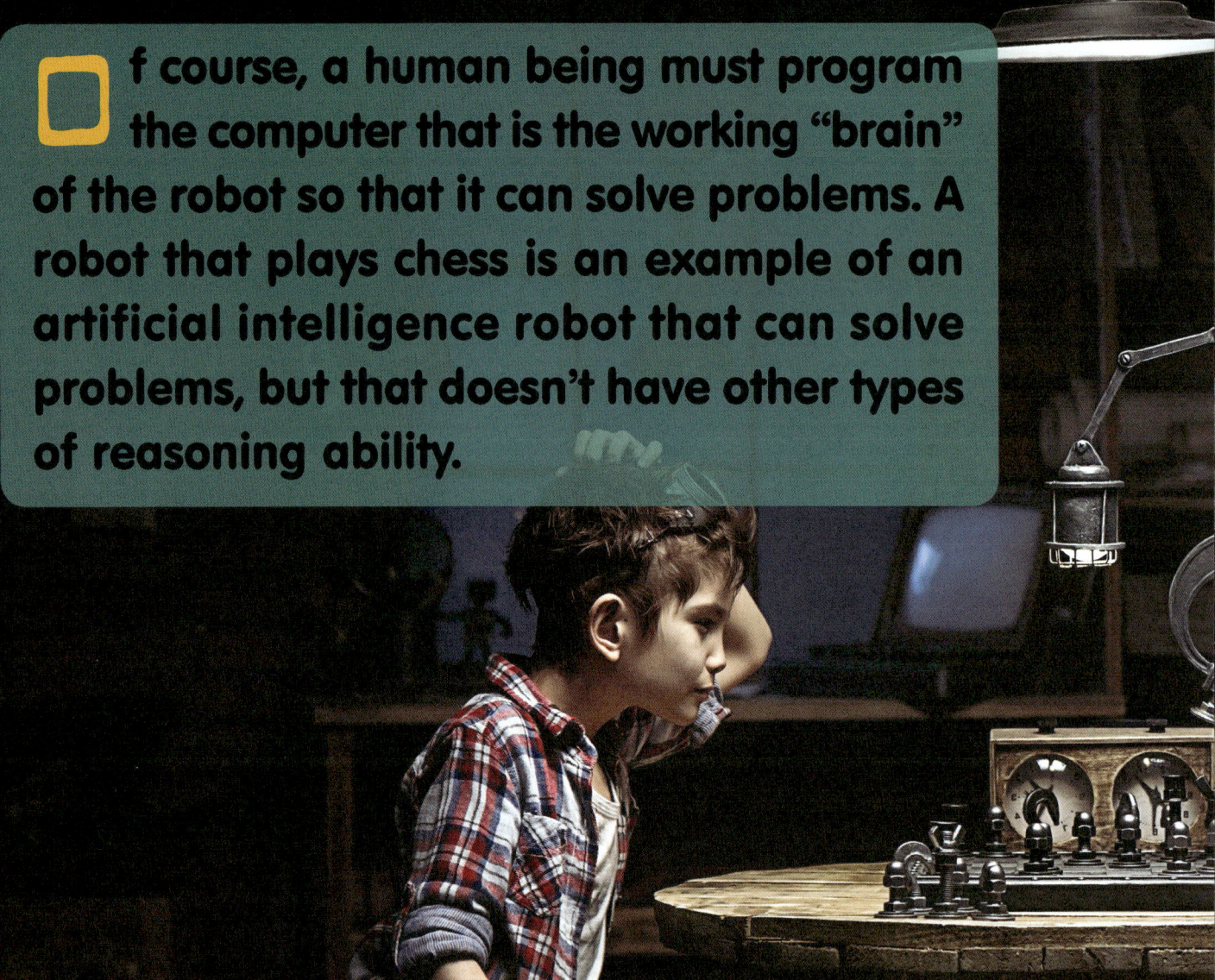

Of course, a human being must program the computer that is the working "brain" of the robot so that it can solve problems. A robot that plays chess is an example of an artificial intelligence robot that can solve problems, but that doesn't have other types of reasoning ability.

CAN ARTIFICIAL INTELLIGENCE ROBOTS LEARN ON THEIR OWN?

Roboticists have already produced robots that can learn, although that learning is limited. Suppose you touch a stove and it's hot and you burn your hand. The next time you get close to the stove, you'll remember that you burned your hand and you'll proceed with caution.

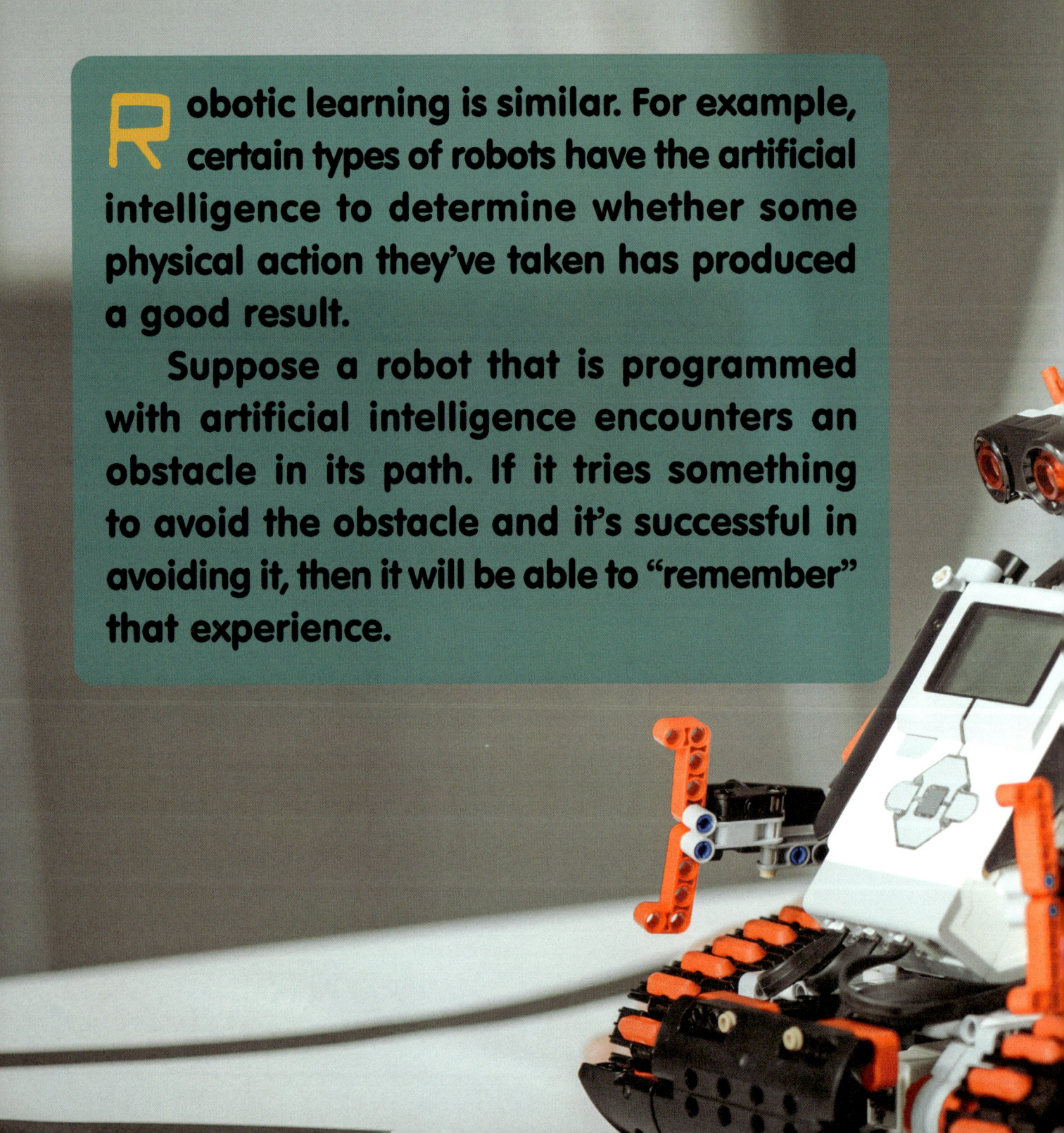

Robotic learning is similar. For example, certain types of robots have the artificial intelligence to determine whether some physical action they've taken has produced a good result.

Suppose a robot that is programmed with artificial intelligence encounters an obstacle in its path. If it tries something to avoid the obstacle and it's successful in avoiding it, then it will be able to "remember" that experience.

A HUMANOID ROBOT TEACHES A MAN THE ART OF DANCING.

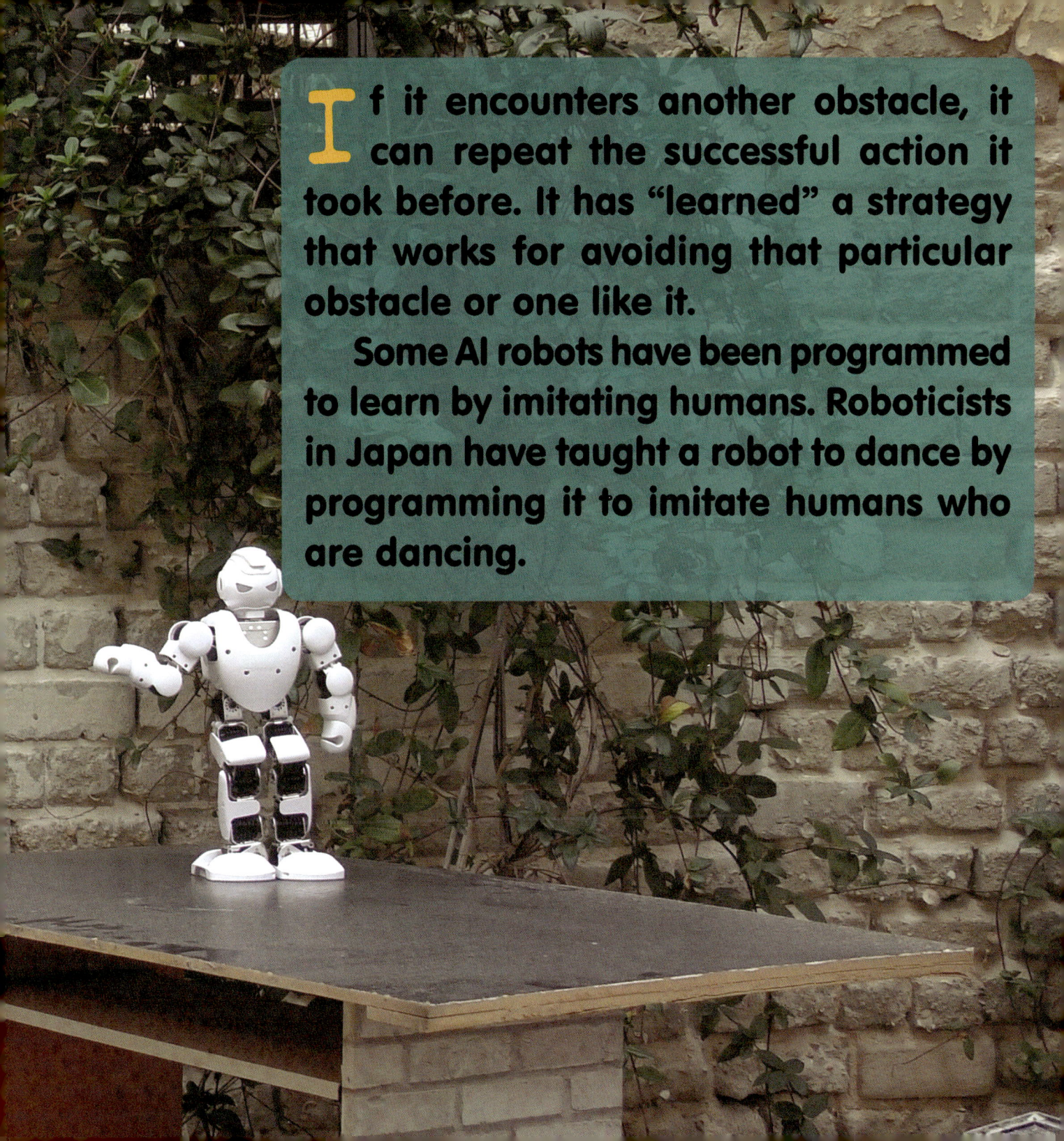

If it encounters another obstacle, it can repeat the successful action it took before. It has "learned" a strategy that works for avoiding that particular obstacle or one like it.

Some AI robots have been programmed to learn by imitating humans. Roboticists in Japan have taught a robot to dance by programming it to imitate humans who are dancing.

CAN ARTIFICIAL INTELLIGENCE ROBOTS BE SOCIAL?

Some robots have been programmed with the artificial intelligence needed to interact with people on a social level. For example, a robotic head called Kismet that is being created and studied at the Massachusetts Institute of Technology (MIT) can interpret a human being's body position, visual cues, and tone of voice to determine how to react.

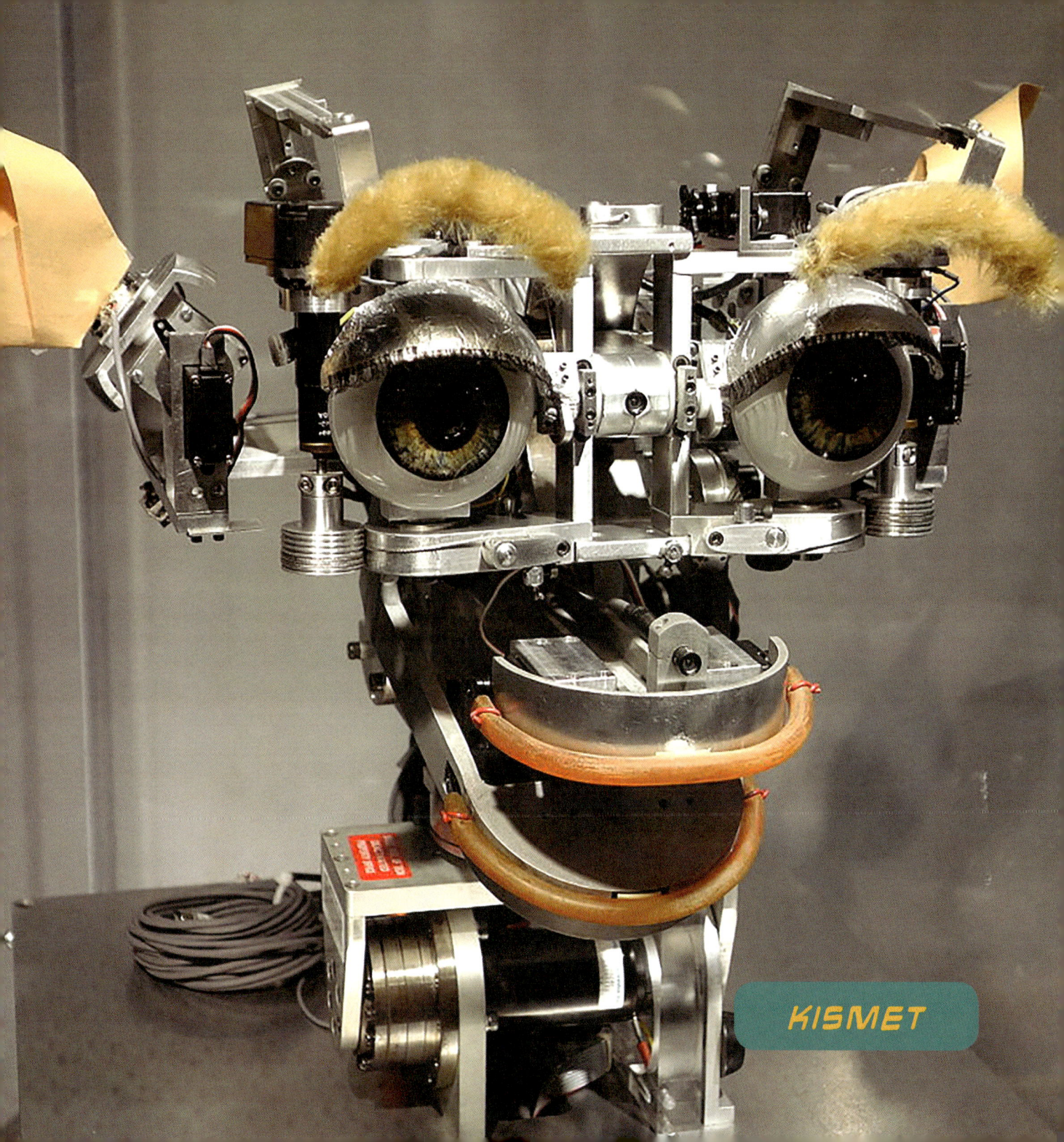

KISMET

The studies at MIT are focusing on the interaction that human beings have with their babies. The human being interacting with Kismet is like its mother or father and Kismet is learning based on their interactions. It takes a host of computer systems and several different operating systems to get Kismet to work. It has a very complex camera system that acts as its eyes.

U nlike other AI robots, Kismet has a computer system that depends on lower-level computers for some of its "thinking." The director of the program, Rodney Brooks, believes this is a good model to use because most human beings don't think consciously when they perform certain actions.

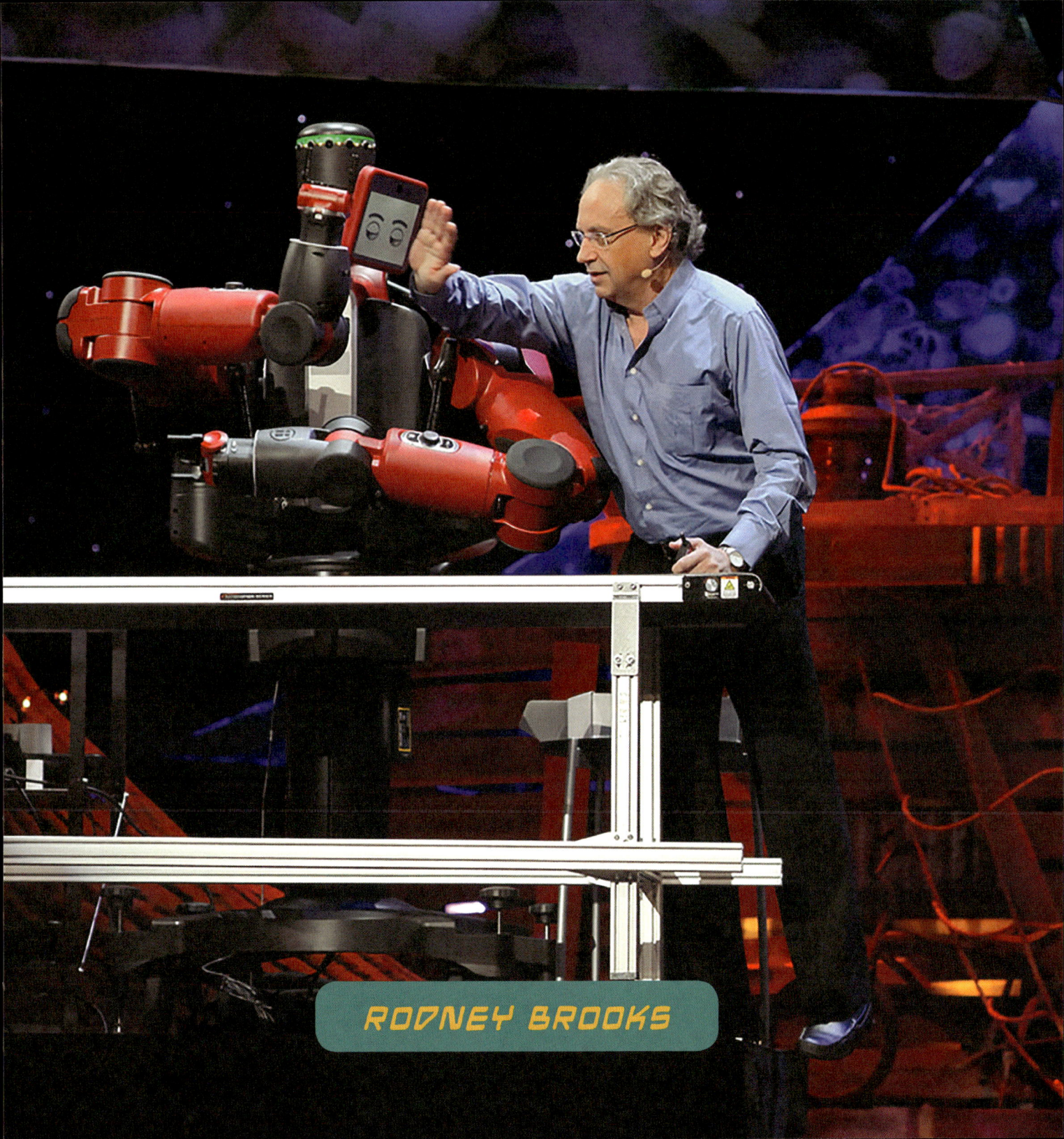

RODNEY BROOKS

For example, if your mom is talking to you, you'd be able to see if she was mad at you or not by watching her face. You could still do this if you were getting a soda out of the refrigerator and pouring it into a glass.

That's because you don't have to do everything with the conscious part of your brain. You don't have to think about:

- I'll walk to the refrigerator.
- I'll take a glass off the shelf.
- I'll grab a can of soda.
- I'll pop open the top.
- I'll pour it into a glass.
- I'll lift it up so I can drink it.

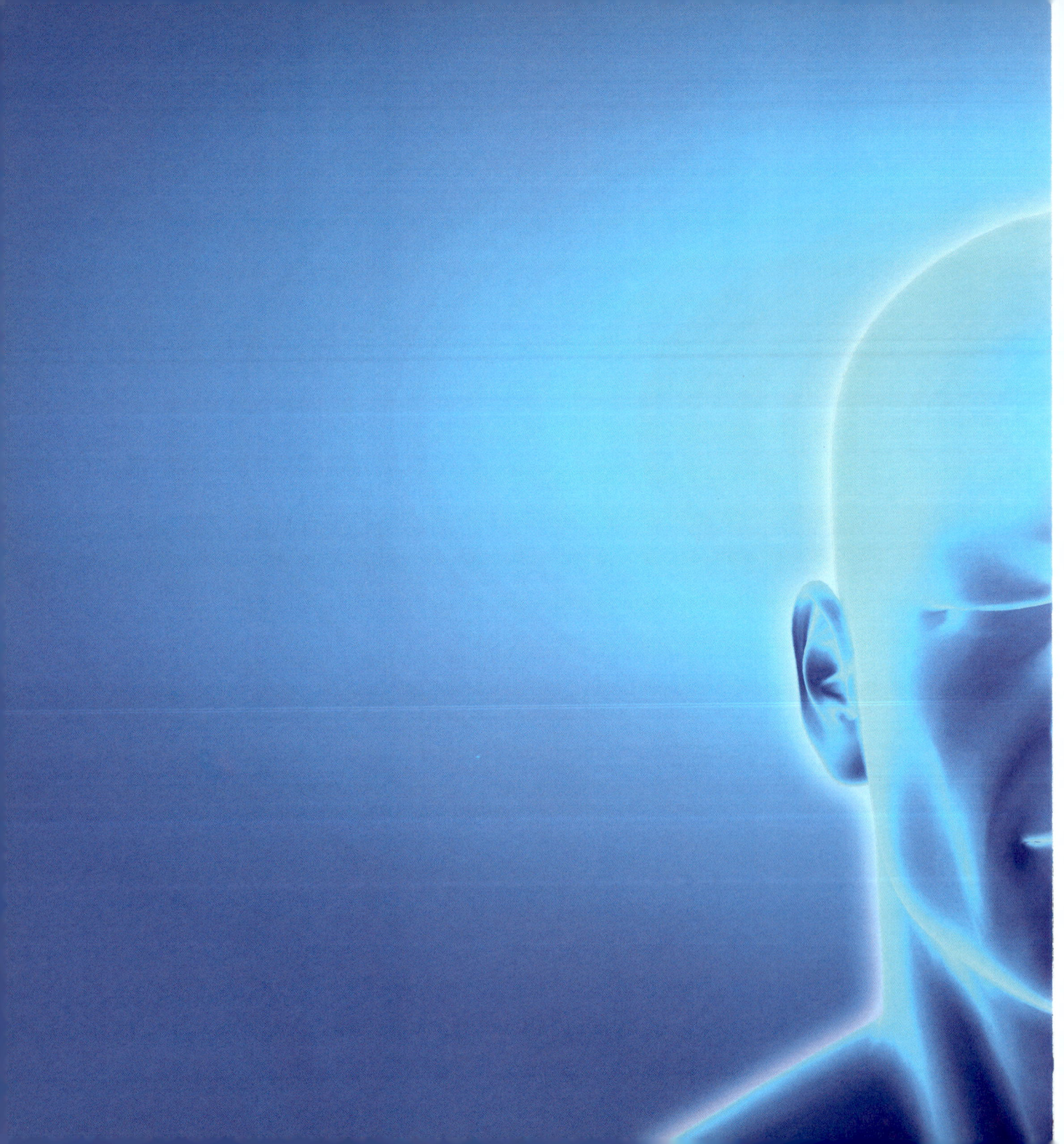

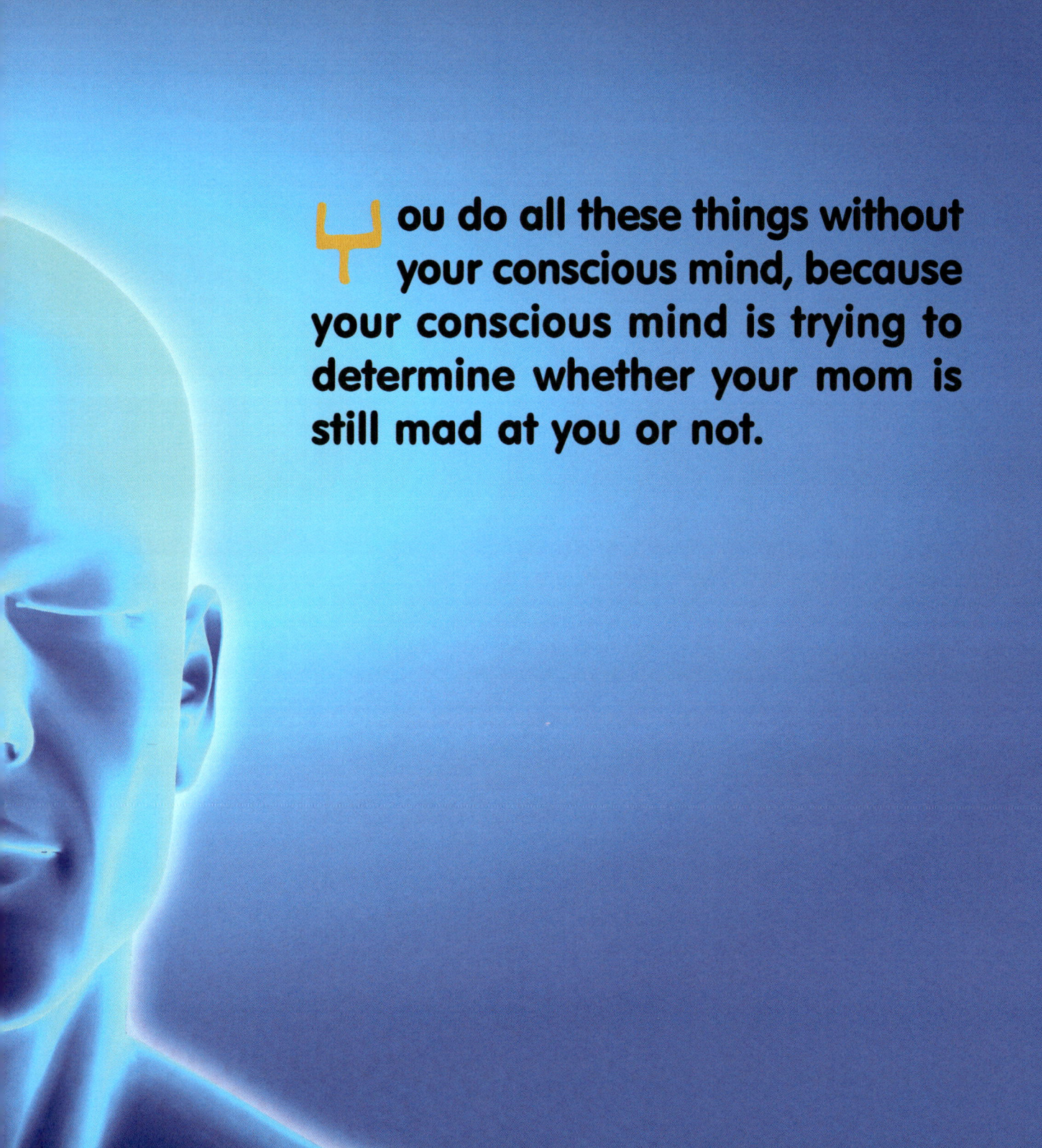

You do all these things without your conscious mind, because your conscious mind is trying to determine whether your mom is still mad at you or not.

CREATING ARTIFICIAL INTELLIGENCE ISN'T EASY

When the artificial heart was invented, physicians knew how the biology of the heart worked. However, to invent a "brain" that works like a human brain works is a much larger challenge.

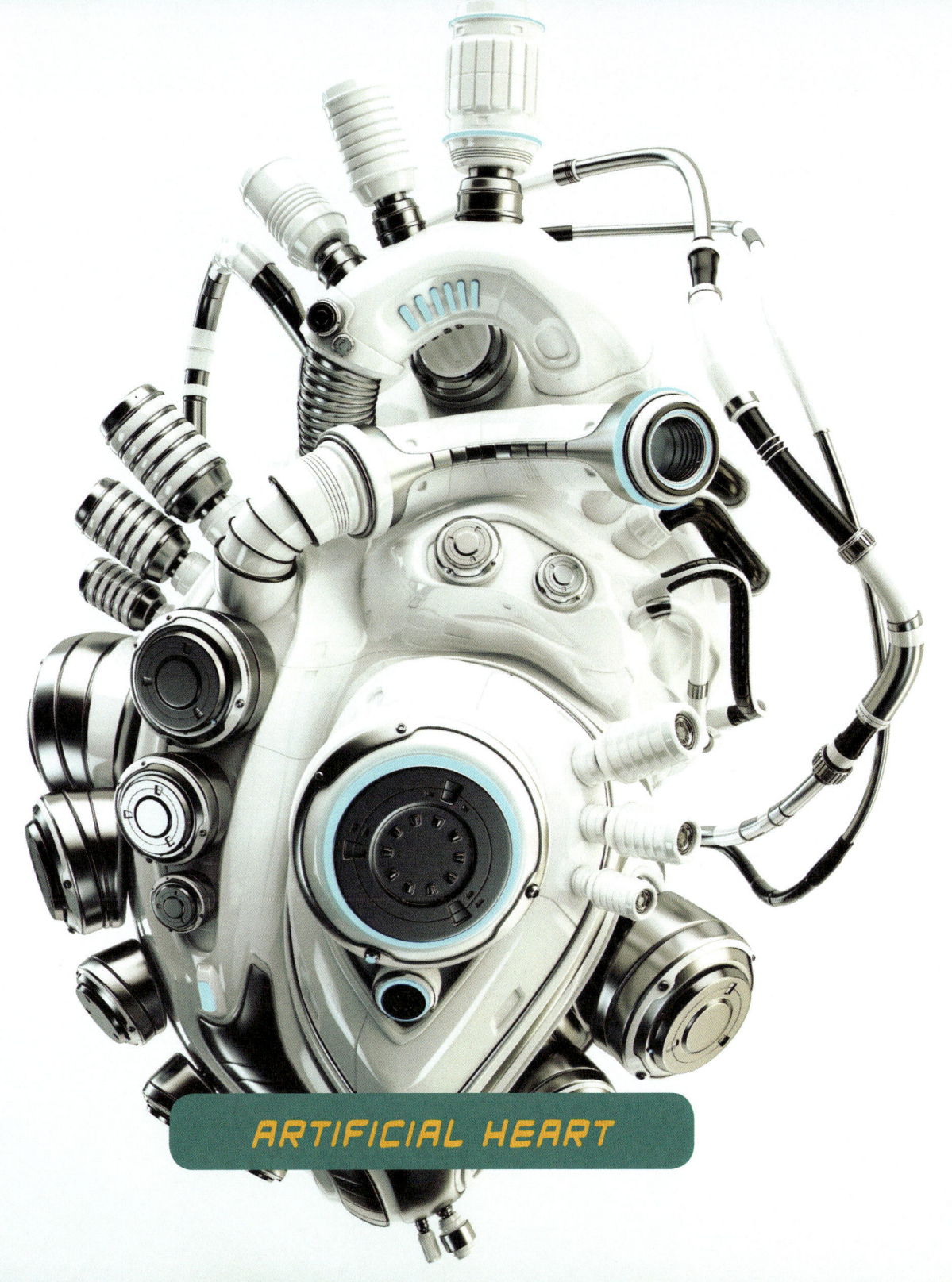

ARTIFICIAL HEART

Scientists know that the human brain contains billions of neurons and that there are electrical pulses between these neurons. They also know in general which areas of the brain are used for which functions. There is still so much that is unknown about how the brain processes information. In fact, every person's intelligence is slightly different since it's based on the experiences that that person has had in life.

This challenge doesn't stop scientists from experimenting with robots and intelligence. In the process, they're learning more about how humans really think. Some roboticists think this is the goal of developing robots with intelligence—it will help us understand our own intelligence.

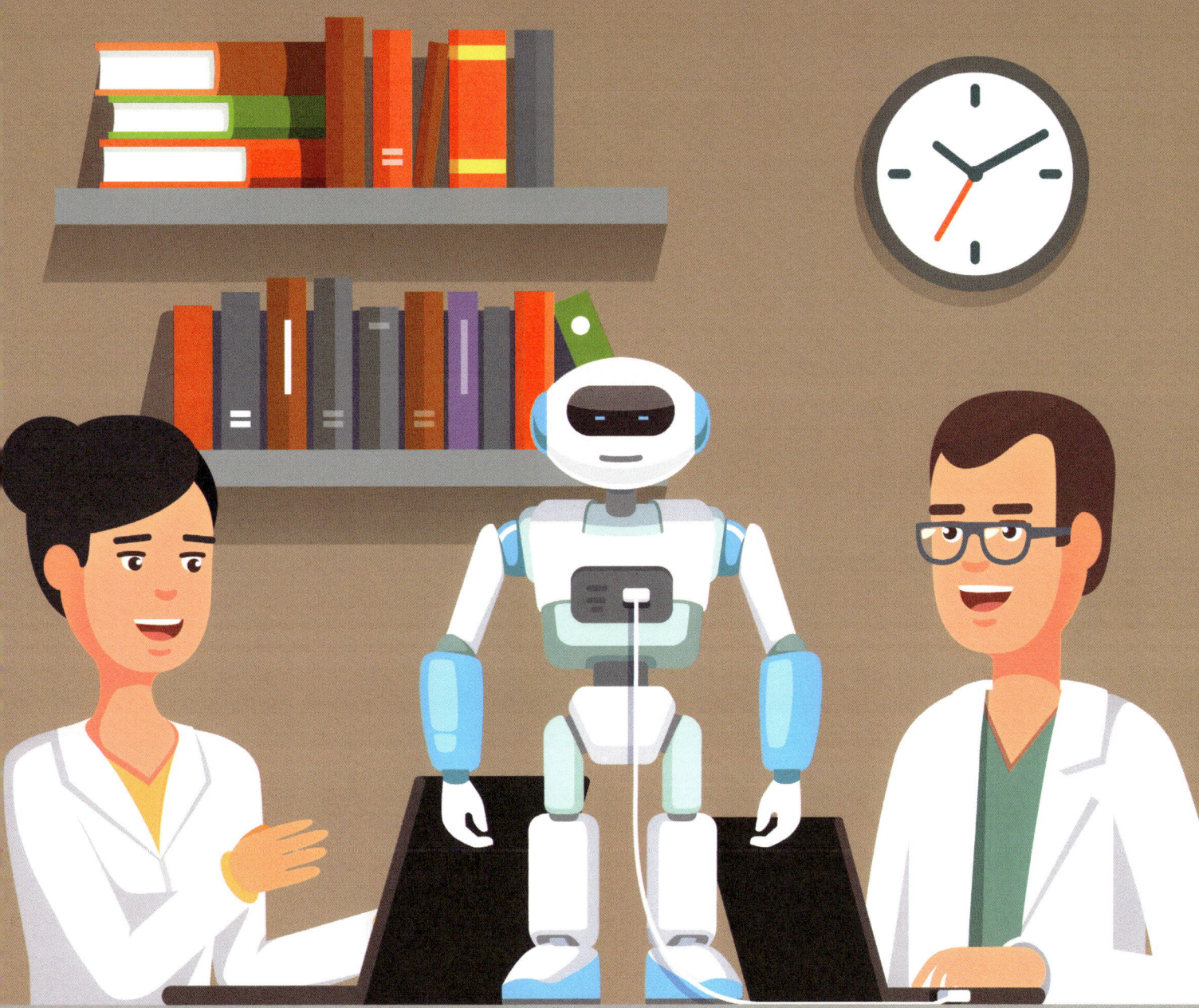

Others believe we will soon work human hand in robotic hand as we work side by side with robots programmed with artificial intelligence. Some future-thinking roboticists believe that human beings will someday integrate their biology with machines. A person's mind loaded into a sturdy, steel robot body could potentially live for thousands of years.

Just as computers moved out of the world of industry and science into people's homes in the 1980s, the same thing will happen with robots within the next few decades. They will start to become part of our daily lives.

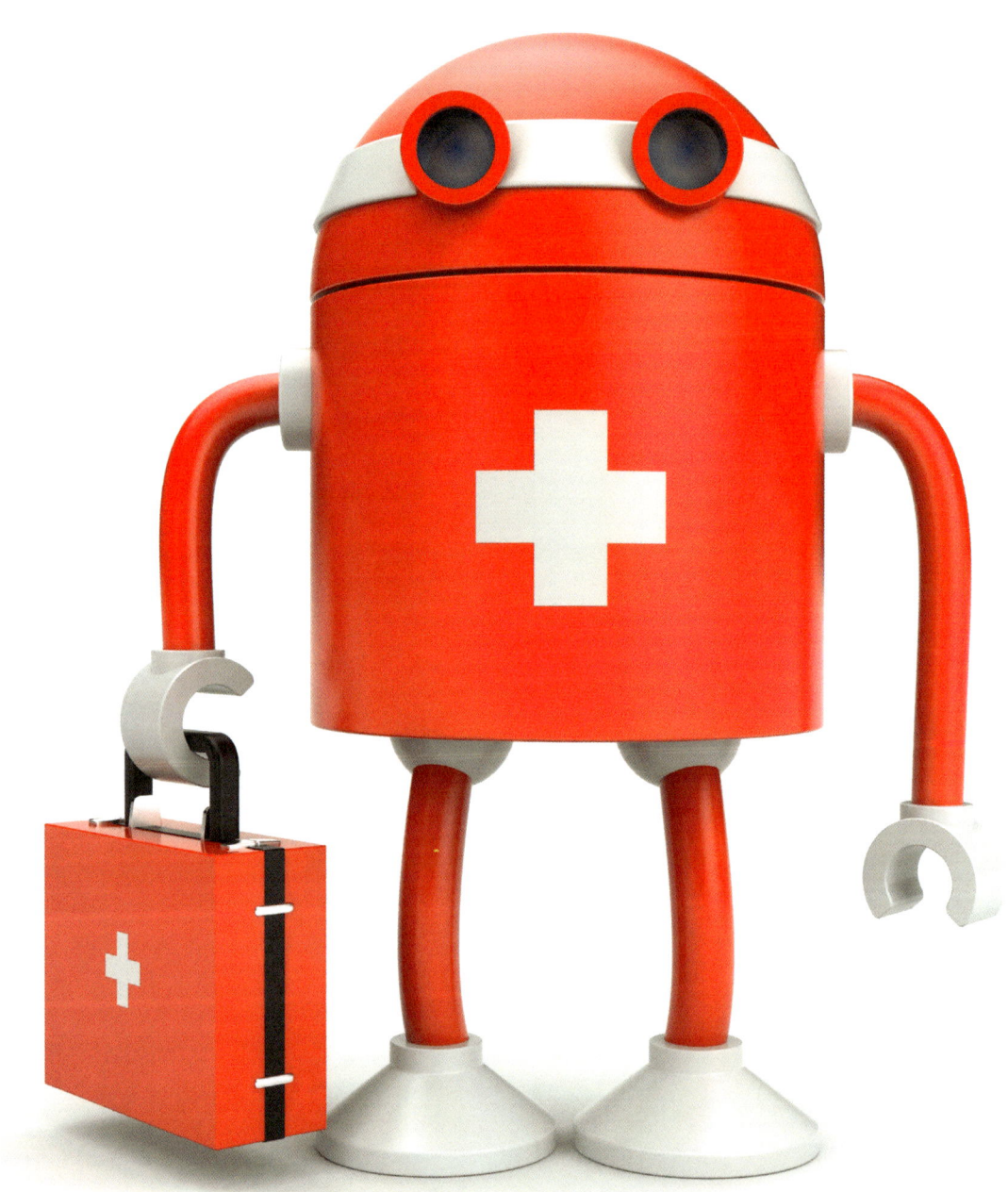

WHAT KINDS OF AI ROBOTS HAVE BEEN CREATED TO DATE?

Artificial intelligence robots have been used as playthings and they've been used to help diagnose illnesses. Here are some of the famous artificial intelligence robots from the last 22 years.

1985

A security company in Boston invented one of the first sentry robots. It was designed as a security guard that would send a radio signal out to a central station. The company wasn't successful. Today, Knightscope is developing new robots designed for patrolling security that are programmed with artificial intelligence.

1988

A toy robot called Furby started a buying frenzy. The cute, fluffy robot was designed to speak a language called "Furbish" but learned commands spoken in English. It "communicated" with other nearby Furbies.

FURBY

ADORABLE TODDLER BOY PLAYING WITH ROBOTIC PET

1999

The Sony Artificial Intelligence Robot, called AIBO for short, was a robotic pet dog. It was able to respond to over 100 different voice commands and was able to talk back to its owners in tones. It could also respond to other AIBOs.

2000

One of the first human-looking robots, Honda's ASIMO, which stands for Advanced Step in Innovative Mobility, was able to walk about a mile. It could even climb stairs and change its direction if there was an obstacle. It could respond to voice commands as well as recognize faces and gestures. About 100 ASIMOs were built.

2002

The Defense Advanced Research Projects Agency, called DARPA for short, built a hundred small robots, called Centibots. They were designed to survey a dangerous piece of land, build a real-time map, and seek out items or people of interest, just like a group of warriors. They communicated as a team and if one wasn't able to perform its mission another one took over. They didn't require any human supervision.

2002

The c was introduced. It cleans a room on its own and can detect and avoid obstacles. It was built based on research from MIT.

ROBOT VACUUM CLEANER

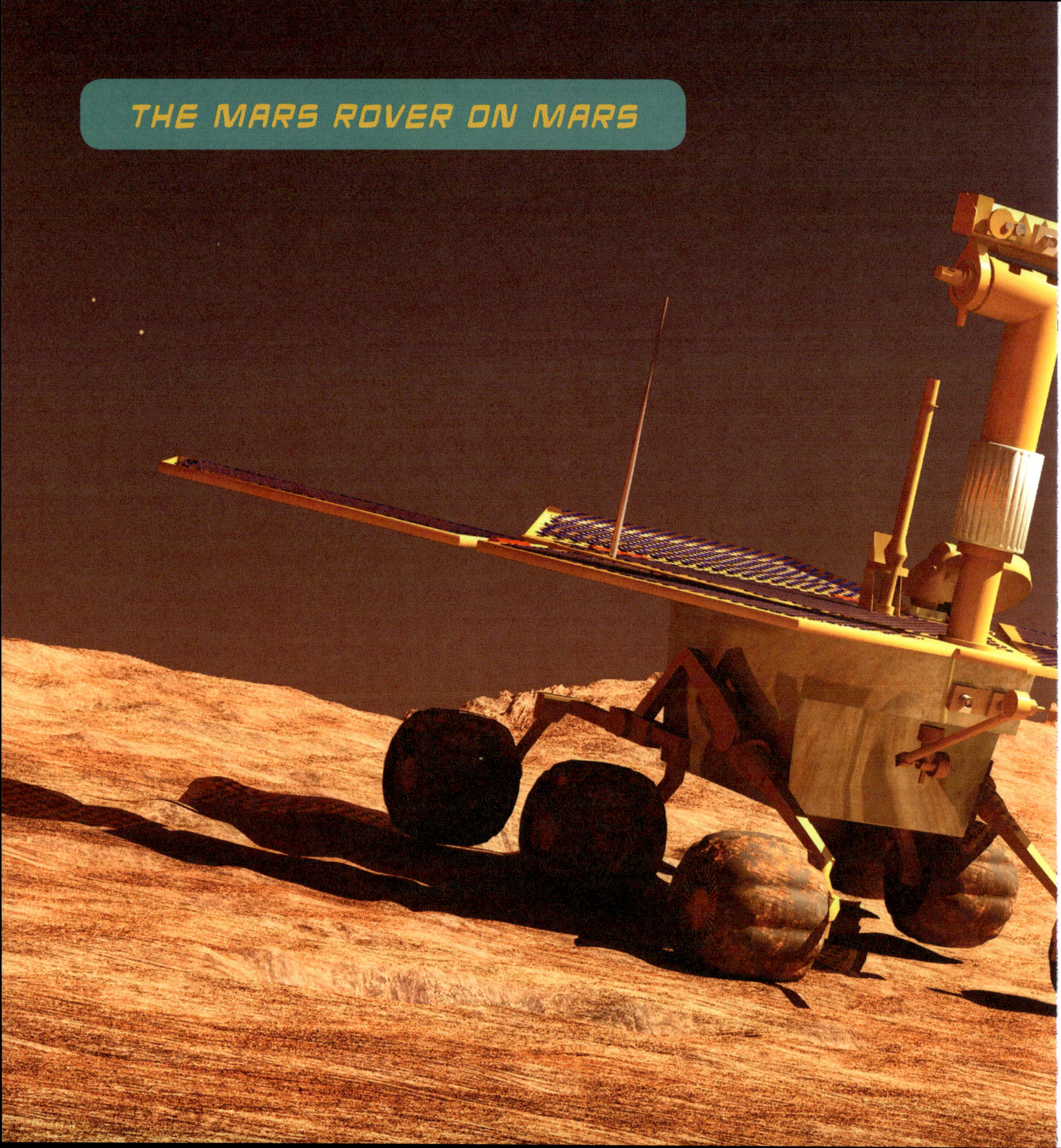

THE MARS ROVER ON MARS

2004

The Mars Rovers, which are robotic vehicles, landed on Mars. They ran way longer than their planned lifetimes and sent valuable information about the Mars environment back to Earth.

2010

IBM's Watson, which some would argue is more computer than robot, beats human contestants at the game—Jeopardy! Today it helps people make accurate medical diagnoses.

Awesome! Now you know more about the different artificial intelligence robots and their uses. You can find more Science Education books from Baby Professor by searching the website of your favorite book retailer.

Visit

BABY PROFESSOR
EDUCATION KIDS

www.BabyProfessorBooks.com

to download Free Baby Professor eBooks
and view our catalog of new and exciting
Children's Books

Printed in Great Britain
by Amazon